BRITAIN IN PICTURES
THE BRITISH PEOPLE IN PICTURES

ENGLISH POTTERY AND PORCELAIN

GENERAL EDITOR
W. J. TURNER

The Editor is most grateful to all those who have
so kindly helped in the selection of illustrations
especially to officials of the various public
Museums Libraries and Galleries and
to all others who have generously
allowed pictures and MSS
to be reproduced

ENGLISH POTTERY
AND
PORCELAIN

CECILIA SEMPILL

WITH
8 PLATES IN COLOUR
AND
29 ILLUSTRATIONS IN
BLACK & WHITE

HASTINGS HOUSE
Publishers   *New York*

PRODUCED BY
ADPRINT LIMITED LONDON
———
SECOND IMPRESSION

PRINTED IN GREAT BRITAIN BY
CLARKE & SHERWELL LTD NORTHAMPTON
ON MELLOTEX BOOK PAPER MADE BY
TULLIS RUSSELL & CO LTD MARKINCH SCOTLAND

LIST OF ILLUSTRATIONS

PLATES IN COLOUR

BLACK AND WHITE ILLUSTRATIONS

SHORT BIBLIOGRAPHY

The Ceramic Art of Great Britain by Llewellyn Tewitt. London 1878
Staffordshire Pottery & Its History by J. C. Wedgwood. London 1914
Catalogue of the Schreiber Collection by Bernard Rackham. London 1928
Old English Porcelain and *English Pottery & Porcelain* by W. B. Honey. London, 1928, 1933

THE WEDGWOOD SHOP, ST JAMES'S STREET, LONDON
Water colour by E. W. Cooke, 1808

THE purpose of this book is not to discuss the merits of the finest examples of English Ceramics, or to compare them with the work of other countries ; rather its aim is to bring to the fore all that is individual in the work of English potters, and all that is peculiar to, and typical of, this country.

Pottery has always been a universal craft, closely allied to the lives of the people and very characteristic of different races. It is indigenous to this country and we have all the essentials here in profusion. The finest clays and ample firing have been generally available, so that the difficulties and expenses which would have been incurred had these to be imported, have not been there to limit the trade. Partly, perhaps, for this reason it has remained an intimate and personal industry, and even when its reputation became world-wide the personal thread never disappeared. This is in strong contrast to most continental pottery when the patronage of wealth so often completely overlaid the intimate peasant character of the ware and produced elaborate masterpieces of ceramic art. Certainly this patronage also produced some lovely work, but from the human point of view it is not nearly so interesting as that which has developed naturally from the day to day demands of ordinary people.

It is undeniably true that the prosperity and self-satisfaction of the nineteenth century had a very unfortunate influence on all craft and industry of that time, and pottery and porcelain suffered with the rest. But one is tempted to observe that even in our worst periods there has been exhibited a humour, unconscious no doubt, but peculiarly native to this country. And through all the ages this humour recurs and gives the feeling that the English potter enjoyed his work, that he potted because he wanted to, because he loved his craft and not just because he had to earn money.

In emphasising the individual character of the work of our potters, it must not be assumed that they worked in a rarified atmosphere, immune to outside influences. This was indeed far from being the case, but foreign influences were mostly soon absorbed and reproduced with a strong native character. A particularly interesting case of this kind is shown in the salt-glaze of the eighteenth century. This particular type of ware is generally supposed to have come to this country originally from Germany in the seventeenth century, but it was rapidly developed here on such lines that it far surpassed anything of the same kind on the Continent, and in fact the eighteenth century salt-glaze made in England is now often considered to be some of the most typical and beautiful ware this country has produced. Later the Chinese influence was very much in evidence here, as in other countries ; but once again it was given a very definite English twist, and though this influence was never so important as salt-glazing, it has left us with some very notable and lovely designs. It probably had a great influence on our own development in porcelain decoration, and brought out our best sense of colour. For in the early English porcelain the colours of the decoration are peculiarly and charmingly our own, even though the symbols are derivative ; and in their directness and simplicity they seem to have a very definite link with the water-colours of Cotman, who was so essentially an English painter.

JUG WITH VERTICAL SLIPWARE DECORATION
From the site of the Bodleian extension, Oxford.   Fourteenth century

BALUSTER JUGS
Green glaze with network pattern. Fourteenth century

FIRST DISTINCTIVE SHAPES

It is not until the thirteenth century that we begin to find really distinctive shapes in our native pottery. Before that time it would be easy to confuse the pots made here with those of many other countries, not excluding oriental work. This similarity was surely not due to influence from other lands, but much more likely it would seem that the early potters all the world over in their beginnings made the same shapes and used the same decorations because they were the easiest to do. Just as amateur draughtsmen usually find it more easy to draw faces looking to the left, so it is likely that the unskilled potters found certain shapes came more easily to their hands.

With the thirteenth century, though not many examples exist, we find very definite and characteristic slender jugs, undecorated except for a green or yellow glaze. In the fourteenth and fifteenth centuries these develop into fine sturdy shapes with applied decorations in the form of rosettes and diaper patterns in different coloured clays. The decorations are often extraordinarily rich in effect, and the scale and placing of the designs shows a remarkable sculptural sense. Some of the under-glaze paintings in simple brush-work sweeps, are masterly in their restraint and decoration ; but it is in the shapes of the vessels themselves that the real character is found. They are robust, generous and hearty and seem to be typical of Chaucer's England.

With the sixteenth century we have the so-called "Cistercian" ware in which we see the beginnings of slipware, which was later so richly developed. The Cistercian ware is notable for its curiously metallic black glaze, and the workings towards slipware in the simple patches of different coloured clay applied under the glaze. Tankards, mugs and tygs (tall, somewhat trumpet-shaped mugs with several handles) are the usual shapes, and they are called "Cistercian" from the fact that most, though not all specimens, have been found on abbey sites. The monks were fine potters in those days, and there are also some good examples of their tiles still in existence. These are often heraldic in decorative form and a favourite method was to inlay the pattern in different coloured clay by an impressed method, probably done with wood blocks.

CISTERCIAN WARE BEAKER WITH TWO HANDLES
Dark brown lead glaze. Sixteenth or seventeenth century

11

SLIPWARE

The slipware of the seventeenth and eighteenth centuries is of immense importance in the study of English ceramics. This method of work reached a height of skill and excellence in this country which it never attained elsewhere. Most of the specimens still existing are obviously the show pieces of the potters, made for some special occasion, such as a wedding perhaps or christening, as an outlet to compensate for the duller everyday work. Little of the ordinary utility ware is left, though we have reason to know that this too was of a high standard in simple design, though it had comparatively little decoration. The show pieces were things of sheer delight, and in them we see all the humour and imagination of the potter who loved his work. There is a fantastic freedom of imagination which reminds one of the gargoyles and pew seats of the

STAFFORDSHIRE SLIPWARE
Mug excavated at Burslem probably made by J. or R. Simpson, c. 1690
Tankard of *sgraffito* slipware, c. 1725

medieval sculptor, and indeed it is likely that these latter were in the same way an outlet for the sculptor as the posset-pots and loving cups were for the potter.

As W. B. Honey so rightly says, the technique of this ware is very similar to that used in decorating an iced cake. Different coloured slips were trailed on the pot in scrolls, arabesques, dots, "stitching" and all manner of ways in most intricate and subtle designs, and afterwards glazed. There certainly is an almost edible quality about some of the most richly decorated pieces, though again the simpler ones, notably the dishes of the Tofts, which usually have some central figure surrounded by more formal patterns, are masterly in execution and sureness of design which though unsophisticated are utterly convincing and satisfying. Many different coloured slips were used, and though the more usual are red, white, black and different shades of brown, there is also occasionally a very attractive olive green. The use of counterchange in colours was highly ingenious, and remarkable skill is shown in the handling of the patterns.

The names most prominently associated with this work are those of George Richardson and Nicholas Hubble, and also of course the Toft brothers. The first two worked at Wrotham in Kent, and until Dr. Glaisher made extensive researches in this neighbourhood the names of the Wrotham potters were all unknown and "Wrotham wares" covered this particular class of work, which ranged from approximately 1612 to 1721. Wrotham ware is on the whole less skilful than the Staffordshire slipware, and the total effect is more cakelike and less pictorial. Certain "stitching," probably meant to resemble stump-work, is peculiar to this district and applied rosettes and pads of clay cut into flower and star forms are much used. The Staffordshire slip-workers used a greater variety of coloured clays and were apt to be more pictorial in their designs, particularly on the large dishes usually associated with Thomas and Ralph Toft. These last potters reached the highest peak of slipware, and some of the pieces attributed to them show an incredible skill in the handling of this very difficult process of decoration, quite apart from a fine sense of design. There is a freedom of line in the Staffordshire work which is very distinctive from the Wrotham wares.

Another group of the same type of work is generally known as "Metropolitan" ware from the fact that the pieces have generally been found in or near London. The decoration is much more simple than that of either Wrotham or Staffordshire, and pious texts are usually combined with simple flower designs. It was made roughly during the middle part of the seventeenth century, but seems to have finished with the great fire of 1666.

In Staffordshire particularly there were various other methods of using slip apart from the icing-sugar technique, and "feathering" and "combing" were particularly effective. Both these were very similar in method and result to the marbled papers used in book-binding and some of the pieces are extraordinarily lovely. "Agate" ware, yet another process used about this time, was a mixing of different coloured clays in the body of the pot so that the effect was not unlike those lumps of plasticine which are composed of the odds and ends of various coloured sticks. On the whole not very attractive, though some of the bolder pieces have charm. Finally there was the incised method, when the design was scratched through the outer slip to a contrasting body ; or in some cases large areas of outer slip were cut away to leave as it were a stencilled pattern underneath. Altogether it was an exciting period for the potters, and their work was full of imagination and invention.

FULHAM AND NOTTINGHAM STONEWARE AND LAMBETH ENAMELLED EARTHENWARE
Seventeenth and eighteenth century

MAIOLICA AND DELFT WARE

We must now turn to an important type of work which overlapped the slipware period. This is tin-enamelled or maiolica and delft ware and as the names imply these were of Italian and Dutch origin, though the best of this class of work was essentially English in character, and the names maiolica and delft are now only used to distinguish between polychrome and monochrome tin-enamelled decoration respectively.

15

Tin-enamelling is roughly a process of lead-glazing low-fired earthen-ware, with the lead-glaze whitened and made opaque by oxide of tin. This is then painted before firing, and though the range of colours is somewhat limited, it is brilliant compared with anything used in this country before.

The earliest examples of this ware are curiously enough more unlike their foreign counterparts than much which came later, and the sturdy silver mounted jugs (the silver mounts dated about the middle of the sixteenth century) enamelled in deep blue or splashed in purple, brown or yellow, are very typical of this country. Later the maiolica potters who settled in Lambeth and those parts worked in a much more Italian manner, and it was not until nearly a century later that the enamelled ware of our potters showed its true development on lines independent of foreign influences.

At first both colours and designs were very derivative and the English potters were evidently feeling their way with a dazzlingly bright new range of colours hitherto unknown to them. Even so the shapes of the pieces were distinctive and personal, and the barrel-shaped mugs, two handled and lidded posset-pots, and narrow necked pot-bellied wine bottles were peculiar to this country.

Perhaps the best known maiolica wares, which are associated with Lambeth, are those usually decorated with styalised flowers and pictures of the Fall, the latter drawn with much unsophisticated humour. The later Bristol wares, which seem to reach the highest point in this class and period of work, include portraits and hunting scenes on these typical large dishes or chargers, and better still there are from the same town lovely posset-pots, bowls and tiles decorated in monochrome, usually blue or purple.

But perhaps the loveliest of all this ware as made in England is found in the so-called Bristol Delft, which combines the technique of tin-enamelling with strong Chinese influence on the design. Perhaps it is more accurate to say Chinese inspiration, for the designs though certainly inspired by the orientals would never have been executed by them. Once again we have an unmistakably English approach to the subject, and the freedom of thought and drawing quite apart from the use of colour, are all our own, as may be seen particularly in the first half of the eighteenth century. Here we have dishes, punch bowls and table-ware decorated with the most charmingly romantic landscapes in which stroll, as it were, oriental or Gainsborough-like figures. Amongst the little houses, trees and lakes, boats and people come and go, sometimes in blue or purple alone, and sometimes in the most surprisingly bright colours with a particularly noticeable clear red.

The Liverpool-Delft ware was on the whole not nearly so interesting, though, in passing, mention must be made of the very typical punch-bowls

16

SLIPWARE DISH BY THOMAS TOFT, C. 1675

The design shows, though incorrectly, the Royal Arms of England. The initials C.R. stand for Charles II

By courtesy of the Fitzwilliam Museum, Cambridge

STAFFORDSHIRE TEAPOT DECORATED WITH APPLIED RELIEFS, C. 1755

From the Glaisher collections

from these parts, mostly made in the eighteenth century, with topical inscriptions and coats of arms. At Liverpool they also used transfer-printing on tiles, which though not very pleasing in effect is historically not unimportant. Much Liverpool ware is of disputed origin ; the best is apt to be claimed as Bristol, and on the whole this seems likely to be true.

Mention must be made of that charming group of wine bottles which come into the Delft class. These mostly date from the middle of the seventeenth century and are usually only decorated with the name of the wine and possibly the date, and an arabesque or flourish usually in blue or purple. The lettering is completely adequate as decoration, and these bottles are amongst some of the most delightful and typical English tin-enamelled ware.

ENAMELLED EARTHENWARE PAINTED IN BLUE
WITH PORTRAITS OF TWO CHILDREN
Inscribed on the back—E. A. Taylor, Bristol
Middle of the eighteenth century

THE BEGINNINGS OF STONEWARE

John Dwight of Fulham (1637 to 1703) is one of the important single figures in the history of ceramics in this country ; not on account of the beauty of his productions, for though there are many excellent pieces which come under his name it is now generally agreed that these were made by others working under his direction. The fame of Dwight rests on the fact that it was he who first introduced stoneware into this country. In 1671 he took out his first patent for stoneware, which up till then seems not to have been made in England at all. From the Dwight works in Fulham now comes an entirely new class of work which was later to be developed into one of the finest and most individual classes of English pottery. Stoneware is merely pottery fired at a very high temperature, which makes it extremely hard and impervious to liquids. But its true beauty and usefulness was found when it was salt-glazed (through salt being thrown into the kiln at the height of the firing) which added a very hard film of glaze to the objects in the kiln.

Very little remains that can be attributed with certainty to Dwight, though the most important and interesting pieces without doubt came from his works. These are of course the salt-glaze busts and figures which show a perfection of technique for ceramic statuary. One of the reasons why so few pieces remain is due to the fact that each bust or figure was the actual work of the artist and was not duplicated in any way. The very hardness of this ware was particularly suitable for the clear cut forms of sculpture, and the thin salt-glaze gave a most attractive liveliness to the surface. Most of these figures are of a white or slightly buff colour (also an innovation of Dwight's) though there are one or two examples in dark brown, which is the colour with which salt-glaze is usually associated nowadays. The most charming figure of all is that inscribed "Lydia Dwight dyed March 3rd 1673," a half-length recumbent figure of a child modelled with touching simplicity and feeling. However, it is not to be assumed that even this was the work of Dwight himself, though it undoubtedly came from his factory. The name of the sculptor is not known with any certainty, but the present opinion seems to be that it may have been the young and then unknown Grinling Gibbons.

In 1693 Dwight brought a lawsuit against John and David Elers and others for infringement of patents in connection with his processes, and this is another important landmark in this story. The Elers brothers who were of Dutch-German origin, started their lives as silversmiths and then later learned the art of stoneware in Cologne. Having sound business instincts, and seeing the great possibilities of this ware, they came to England and settled first in London, where they started to work. Later they moved to Staffordshire where ample clay and firing were ready to hand, which made it a more suitable centre for pottery. Their appearance

'ELERS' WARE
The cup probably by Elers, c. 1695. The teapot c. 1750

in Staffordshire was to prove of the utmost importance, for they not only introduced salt-glaze to that district but also taught the advantages of refining and mixing the clay body, and then the thinness and precision which could be obtained by turning. They in no way competed with Dwight in the making of busts and figures, but where they most successfully encroached on his ground was in the matter of what was known as Dwight's "red porcelain," which was in fact a fine red stoneware, unglazed and of hard texture. This was made to imitate the so-called Chinese red porcelain, which at that time was being imported into this country, and as used by the Elers brothers for tea-pots and the like, it had an immediate success.

The shapes of the tea-pots and mugs attributed to these brothers often show the influence of their silversmith training, but a new lightness and thinness was also brought into the working of clay which was a very important step forward. The hard, tough body could be turned with precision on the lathe, and its same toughness made it very suitable for the applied decorations of sprigs and sprays of flowers and occasionally heads and figures which are so characteristic of the Dwight-Elers work. Staffordshire had now indeed come to the threshold of a new era which was to lead to a lasting world-wide reputation.

19

STAFFORDSHIRE SALT-GLAZE PEW-GROUP
White with brown decoration. Early eighteenth century

THE RISE OF STAFFORDSHIRE FAME

With the Elers brothers an entirely new field had opened, which could compete in quality with the imported Chinese wares in such demand owing to the rising popularity of tea-drinking. The potters were inspired to experiment and work for a suddenly growing market, and salt-glaze was an exciting new process. Always now the working was towards something akin to porcelain, not only in texture but also in colour, and the next step naturally became white stoneware, the Staffordshire salt-glaze which in its class is unsurpassed to-day.

Before the true white-bodied stoneware appeared, the ordinary clay was surface-washed with a white Devonshire clay (which was non-plastic and so not suitable for making bodies) in a manner similar to the process of tin-enamelling. This innovation is usually ascribed to Astbury (died 1743) though there are varying opinions on this point, as also on the question of who first introduced calcined flint into the clay itself so as to give a white body. This too is now generally thought to have been Astbury's innovation, and by 1730 white stoneware had really come to stay. Shortly after this the use of porous moulds for casting (a method imported from France) caused the Staffordshire wares to take another bound forward and opened up yet another line of development. By this process it was possible to make much thinner and lighter bodies than before, and at the same time much more complicated shapes, such as

STAFFORDSHIRE SALT-GLAZED STONEWARE
Middle of the eighteenth century

could not have been thrown on a wheel or turned on a lathe. Added to this it was also possible to reproduce exact copies of certain shapes in large quantities and with rapidity, so that they could be sold at a price which was within the reach of most people and far below that of imported wares.

The commercialisation of the Potteries was at hand ; all the ingredients were there, and at this point Josiah Wedgwood came on the scene and by his masterly direction established the fame of the Potteries, not only at home but abroad. But here we must go back a little, for the rise of Wedgwood marks the end of the salt-glaze period, and this period produced some of the most beautiful and most typical work of English potters, and cannot be dismissed without further comment.

Nottingham salt-glaze, which flourished from the beginning of the eighteenth century until nearly the end, stands in a class by itself. It is curiously uninfluenced by Staffordshire, and has a sculptural simplicity about its shapes which are all its own. Most of the pieces are of a warm brown colour, and the decorations are usually incised formal flower patterns or even more usually simple cross-hatchings and patterns not unlike the pargettings of the old Essex plaster walls ; dates are often included and all this is placed with the utmost restraint and in no way confuses the noble and dignified shapes ; two-handled loving cups, bowls and mugs, were all made with a lightness which again distinguishes it from other salt-glaze of that time.

STAFFORDSHIRE ENAMELLED SALTGLAZED STONEWARE. MIDDLE OF THE EIGHTEENTH CENTURY
Toy teapot with red rose design on a black ground

On returning to Staffordshire we find that Astbury's white washes and white clay bodies had inspired a use of colour which had not been employed on stoneware before. The white grounds lent themselves to painted decoration which gave further opportunities to compete with the gaily decorated imported porcelains.

One of the first uses of white salt-glaze was in contrast with coloured clays, and so we have an interesting development from the earlier slip-ware. Now we find sprigging, vining, rosettes and stamped reliefs in white on coloured bodies, and the results are often very charming indeed. Astbury's name is associated with much of this work, but Thomas Whieldon (1719 to 1795) developed his ideas further. Whieldon made great use of "agate" ware for bodies, which though technically interesting were not always very beautiful. But we find his most attractive development in his lead-glaze ware on which he combines a number of fine coloured glazes with moulded and applied reliefs in "vineing" and stylised flower spriggings. The colours of this typical Whieldon-ware (most often in teapot form) are strong and rich and mark an important advance in coloured decoration. Whieldon also made some birds and figures very charmingly decorated and glazed in these same colours.

But of all Staffordshire figures the most interesting and most typical of this time, or perhaps any time, were the famous pew-groups of the first half of the eighteenth century. There are not a great number of them in all, and it is thought that they may all have been the work of Aaron Wood, a famous block-cutter of that time, who started work as an apprentice to Thomas Wedgwood in 1731. These stylised figures have all the charm and humour of the Toft brothers' slip-ware, and the child-like simplicity of approach has a directness which is completely satisfying for the material used. These groups are usually in white salt-glaze picked

22

out most amusingly in brown slip. Seated figures of couples smirk at each other in their pews or gaze ahead with embarrassed aloofness. The dresses of the period are rendered with intriguing details of buttons, bows and curling wigs. There is a superlative group of the Fall in the Glaisher collection, and the whole story may clearly be read in the expressions of Adam and Eve. Though the figures are naive, the design of the tree and its decorative composition with the whole group is masterly.

The Whieldon-type figures (mid-eighteenth century) are of course coloured, and though they too have a childlike charm they are certainly more sophisticated than the pew-groups, and seem to have a slightly oriental character. The coloured groups attributed to Ralph Wood (second half of the eighteenth century) and much sought after to-day are more mature still, and though they have humour it is not as spontaneous as that of the earlier pew-groups. The colours however are lovely and very individual, though the figures themselves are often copied from French groups or even engravings. This same Ralph Wood was of course primarily famous for his Toby jugs; but these too are now thought to have been inspired, or even originally modelled by a Frenchman. The salt-glaze stoneware enamelled in colours, again in emulation of the imported oriental porcelain, once more takes a bound forward and some pieces now clearly show their workings towards the first English porcelain designs. William Duesbury, who later made porcelain at Derby, was previous to that known to have decorated salt-glaze ware for Staffordshire. There are some good pieces (again mainly tea and punchpots) attributed to him and his workers, dating between 1750 and 1760, in which the oriental flowers and figures are given a new and personal life and vitality.

Shortly after this, transfer printing began to be used with salt-glaze. In its initial stages it was very charming, and the colours were used sparingly and effectively, and the transfers themselves were placed with a sure sense of design. It was later of course that this type of decoration became so debased, when it was plastered on at random by people who had no eye for design and only had an urge for more and more ornament.

STAFFORDSHIRE 'WHIELDON' WARE TEAPOT
Agateware, 1750-1760

23

WEDGWOOD

DETAIL FROM A CATALOGUE ISSUED BY JOSIAH WEDGWOOD
IN THE EARLY NINETEENTH CENTURY
Plate engraved by William Blake

JOSIAH WEDGWOOD
AND THE SOPHISTICATION OF POTTERY

As has been noted before, the rise of Wedgwood marks the decline of salt-glaze, for Josiah Wedgwood's cream earthenware was from every point of view a better commercial proposition than the white salt-glaze, and Wedgwood was certainly a very good business man quite apart from his other qualities.

It is fashionable nowadays to deplore the commercialisation of the Potteries as being the death of true ceramic art in this country, but this is a very short sighted view of the true case. Sophistication, commercialisation, industrialisation had to come, as inevitably as middle age must follow youth unless the youth dies young. And as this development was inevitable so were we lucky to have it brought about primarily by a man of such high standards as Josiah Wedgwood. The texture and quality of his cream earthenware from about 1760 until the present day has been unsurpassed, or for that matter, unequalled ; and his simpler shapes from then until now, have always shown an appreciation of what the ordinary people needed, and they were given it in the very best forms. Wedgwood's work has been much obscured by the exotic demands of the mid-Victorian era, but even when his firm was turning out the most extravagantly vulgar of their pieces (and they were never as vulgar as those of other potters) at the same time it will be found there was also a steady flow of excellent, simple tableware, of first-class design and quality, to fulfil the everyday needs of ordinary people.

At the end of the eighteenth century there was great demand and scope for new tableware. The white salt-glaze which had been so successful had its drawbacks. It was very brittle, and its great hardness wore away silver spoons and forks. The new cream earthenware had not these disadvantages, and it had a smoother surface which was more suitable for table use. Its success was immediate and its influence wide-spread,

24

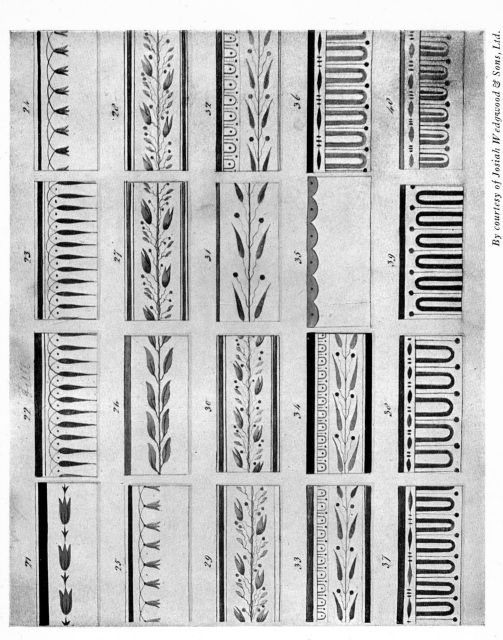

PATTERNS FOR TABLEWARE

Designs from the first pattern book of Josiah Wedgwood begun shortly after 1759

WORCESTER TEAPOT AND BOWL, C. 1765-1770

not only in this country but on the Continent where it achieved a great reputation.

But there was also another way in which Wedgwood made a profound mark on the Potteries, and that was in the improved transport facilities which came about largely through his farsighted and businesslike vision. He it was who agitated until the canal connecting the Trent and Mersey was built, and on July 26th, 1766, he actually cut the first sod of this himself. This means of short-circuiting the transport of clay from Devon and Cornwall, and salt and flints from other parts of the country, reduced the charges per mile to less than one-seventh of what they had previously been.

It may be of interest to mention here also Josiah Wedgwood's connection with James Watt, and his pioneer work in the use of steam power in the Pottery Industry. The first mention of any engine in those parts was that of John Turner of Stoke who employed an engine of sorts, but not a steam engine, to pump water. Spode seems to have bought this later and also used it for pumping. After some experimenting in 1782 and 1784 Wedgwood ordered in 1793 a 10 horsepower steam engine from Watt, to be used for the following purposes : 1. To grind flints. 2. To grind enamel colours. 3. To operate a sagger crusher. 4. To temper or mix clays. This engine was still working up till 1912, when it was demolished and sold for scrap, but it had been the beginnings of all power production in the Potteries.

Leaving the business side of Wedgwood's genius and returning to the wares he produced, we find that as a potter he was infinitely skilful though as an artist he was more persevering than inspired. He produced the most excellently made and designed utility articles, and it is interesting to note that he took great trouble over these simple designs, employing first class men. (We even find that through Flaxman he employed William Blake to draw and engrave the illustrations for the catalogue of shapes in 1815.) He perfected such well known wares as Black Basalt (black unglazed stoneware of extreme hardness and fineness of grain) and Jasper Ware, (a new white body of great hardness, which could be polished on a lapidary's wheel and stained in various colours with metallic oxides). These two wares were largely used for decorative pieces, vases, urns and the like and the famous plaques, cameos and decorative mounts, which were classical in design : sometimes very charming but more often rather dully derivative. The table-ware and intimate little pieces such as buttons, snuff-boxes and beads, were far more interesting and personal.

On the other hand the decoration of his cream earthenware, or Queensware as it is called, even though it was also classical in feeling, showed much more imagination and artistic sense, and many of the early border designs are quite lovely in every way. There was great charm too in his perforated ware, which was later to be developed and copied so success-

1238

Asses milk vessel

1240

Inhaling Pot

ARTICLES FOR USE IN THE SICK-ROOM
From Josiah Wedgwood's first Shape Book

fully at Leeds. It was inevitable that a man of Wedgwood's inventive genius should have many imitators, but not many of them even approached the very high standard of his productions in the perfection of finish on which he insisted, and certainly none was successful in such a variety of techniques in which he excelled. William Adams, John Turner and Henry Palmer were some of those who made jasper, basalt and marbled wares after Wedgwood's patterns. Often they made blatant copies, though sometimes, as in the case of Turner, the designs were more original than the models. The first Josiah Spode naturally owed much to Wedgwood also, but he broke out in an entirely new line in "blue-printed" earthenware. It was in 1770 that he began making printed cream ware, and by 1790 this was the most popular ware produced in the Potteries, and decorated tableware was within the reach of ordinary people. The first printed ware produced by Spode was on glaze in black with the colour (cobalt blue) filled in by hand. Later he learnt from Turner of Worcester the art of under-glaze printing from coloured transfers, not so unattractive when the colour was confined to blue only, as with Spode's ware. He made an enormous fortune from this type of work, and created a fashion for blue and white which dominated the last half of the eighteenth century.

Leeds also took up many of Wedgwood's innovations, but it is principally on that pottery's developments of the pierced cream-coloured ware that its reputation rests. Lovely and delicate tableware came from there from 1774 onwards, and the finely pierced borders and centre pieces are worthy successors to the first of this type of work made by Wedgwood. Between 1760 and 1780 there was also produced some very charming enamelled cream earthenware, notably that in red and black only, which is now almost always attributed to Leeds though Staffordshire claims some too.

At the end of the century much Staffordshire ware was sent to Liverpool to be painted, and it is often very hard to tell which are local productions. Much of this was made for the American market at this time,

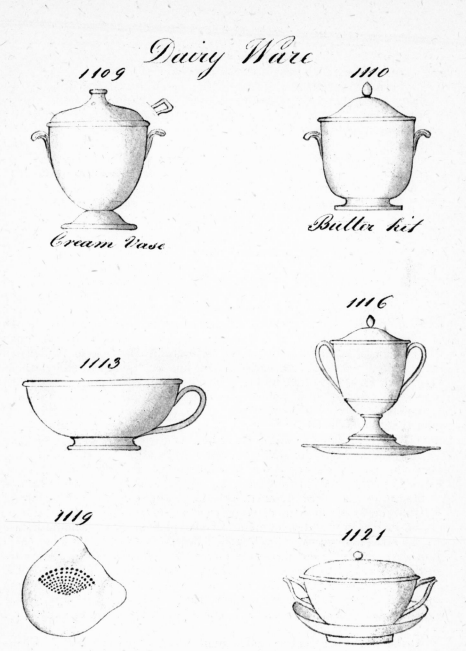

Dairy Ware

1109

Cream Vase

1110

Butter kit

1113

1116

1119

1121

ARTICLES FOR USE IN THE DAIRY
From Josiah Wedgwood's first Shape Book

particularly jugs and mugs with rustic scenes and inscriptions. With the close of the eighteenth century and the development of porcelain, there is an end to the vigorous growth of true pottery in this country. It is true, as has been observed before, that there has always persisted a vein of excellent productions for those who looked for them or needed them, in mass-produced earthenware of such factories as Wedgwood's. But the peasant pottery which was so typically English was swamped by the new fashions and new demands for cheaper, 'prettier' and brighter tableware, which also insisted on a white body ; and we find for a time that the naiveté and charm which seemed to leave earthenware with the industrial-isation of the Potteries, passes to the new discovery of porcelain, until it, too, becomes sophisticated and in its cleverness loses its charm.

STAFFORDSHIRE CREAM-JUG IN BLUE JASPER WARE WITH CAMEO RELIEF IN WHITE
Made by John Turner. Late eighteenth century

EARLY PORCELAIN

Before we go on to the nineteenth century it seems more fitting now to go back a little time to the beginnings of English porcelain.

Porcelain had been made in Europe long before the English potters discovered the secret. It was known in Italy as early as the end of the sixteenth century, but the earliest dated piece known to have been made in England is a Chelsea jug of 1745 (now in the British Museum) though the Bow factory came into existence just before that.

Most English porcelain is what is known as "soft paste" and is, as its name implies, softer and more opaque than true, or "hard paste" porcelain as made in the Far East. Hard paste was only made at Bristol, Plymouth and New Hall. English eighteenth century porcelain is very "peasant" in comparison with contemporary work on the Continent, which was at that time greatly patronised by the nobility and so more sophisticated and elaborate. This continental work was much imitated in England, but in such a fresh and naive way that it took on a new life. Over-glaze painting is the most usual decoration of English porcelain, and printing on porcelain (used most extensively at Worcester) was an English invention perhaps of more interest than merit. The colours used in painting, particularly in early work, were particularly fresh and clean, notably in yellows, emerald green and an excellent purple. The feeling for figures and groups which developed about this time gave great scope for this new material ; and the lively colours, and the fashion for tea-drinking called for new and lighter tableware which could be supplied by porcelain.

Bow is generally accepted as being the earliest porcelain factory set up in this country, and its manager for some time was Thomas Frye, who in 1744 took out a patent for making porcelain in which he used an imported clay from America called unaker. A second patent of his in 1748 mentions the inclusion of what seems most likely to have been calcined bones, and some fifty years later Josiah Spode perfected the use of this bone-ash which came into general use and is still one of the usual ingredients of English porcelain to-day.

In 1768 William Cookworthy of Plymouth took out a patent for making true hard-paste porcelain, but it was an expensive commercial proposition and could not compete with other wares of that date. Cookworthy moved his works to Bristol in 1770 and in 1781 sold his patent rights. Hard paste was made in small quantities for a short time after this at New Hall (Staffordshire) but by 1820 it was no longer made in England.

The Bow factory made much tableware for general use, but it is in fact for its figures that it is probably best known. The earliest Bow pieces, which include figures in plain white porcelain, are of somewhat uneven textured paste with a thick greenish-yellow glaze, and where colours are used they are apt to be rather crude. From about 1755 onwards however, some really lovely work came from this factory. The paste and glaze had improved and extremely skilled modellers and enamellers were employed. A certain Frenchman called Tebo (or Thibaud) who at one time worked for Wedgwood, is known to have worked as a repairer in the Bow factory, and is also thought to be the modeller of some of the early groups marked To. A certain John Bacon was also thought to have been one of their modellers, and J. T. Smith in *Nollekins & his Times* quotes a conversation between Nollekins and Panton Betew in which the former declared that Moser, Keeper of the Royal Academy, modelled also for this factory.

Concerning the enamelling of these pieces there is much speculation and controversy, but it is interesting to find that William Duesbury, who was known as a salt-glaze enameller, also worked independently decorating Chelsea, Bow and other ware. It is not known for certain if he enamelled, or merely decorated in unfired colours, but certain pieces seem to be very typical of his work. Later he bought up the Longton Hall works and started the Derby factory in 1756.

Whoever modelled or enamelled these charming Bow figures, the fact remains that they are some of the best that were ever made in porcelain in this country. They are on the whole simpler and cleaner in form than the Chelsea groups and there is an unusual use of colours, often discordantly lovely, which is very typical. The birds are quite fantastic in their colourings, but the light-hearted invention has all the attractiveness of a fairy tale.

The figure groups were often copies of those from Meissen, but they were simplified and endowed with a new life and character. The tableware on the other hand was more imitative of Oriental decorations, not so well assimilated or translated, though some of the printed decoration and underglaze blue painting is fresh and sprightly. The printed designs are usually of French or Italian influence. There are some lovely plates painted with fruits and flowers, very similar to some from the Chelsea factory, and possibly even done by the same hand.

The later work of this factory showed a great falling off in quality of material and design, and in 1776 it was closed down.

The Chelsea factory is known to have existed in 1745, though it is uncertain how long before that it had been started. It is believed that two Frenchmen called Charles Gouyn and Nicolas Sprimont were the original owners of the works, and certainly the porcelain they made was of the French type of soft paste of a very translucent, creamy quality. Sprimont was a silversmith, which probably accounts for the fact that some of the earliest shapes were derived from silver work. This earliest work is marked with an incised triangle, and the famous "goat and bee" pieces belong to this period.

CHELSEA FIGURE
Boy in red coat, yellow vest and turquoise breeches

About 1750 a denser paste was used and a colder glaze, and the anchor mark first appears, in relief on an oval medallion. Figures and birds began to be made in large quantities, much influenced by Meissen though not direct copies of these subjects. The colours were much more naturalistic than those of Bow. Between 1750 and 1760 some good work came from this factory, both in groups and figures and in table ware. The former are justifiably well-known, though the uncoloured groups are not as generally familiar as the coloured, which is a pity as they show off the thick cool glaze to perfection.

When colour was used it was with immense taste and skill, and the interpretation was essentially English and often more lovely than the originals. The colours of flowers and birds were clean, lively and unexpected, but they never seemed out of place as so often is the case with later paintings on porcelain.

31

Nicolas Sprimont was evidently a man of great taste, for he seems to have taken over the factory entirely about 1750 and under his rule the highest peak of its manufacture was reached. About 1754 we have the first mention of the "Toys" comprising snuff boxes, trinkets, smelling bottles, seals, etc., which achieved a European reputation. These lovely little objects certainly are the essence of all the charm and humour of the best of our porcelain, and are quite unlike anything made elsewhere.

The tablewares of this date are characterised by decoration in the form of scatterings of birds, flowers and insects in an irregular and light-hearted manner, and are typical of the popular idea of Chelsea china. At the same time were made those plates with large botanical paintings of flowers and fruits with butterflies and insects amongst them. These are some of the loveliest productions of this factory, with their bright, sharp colourings, improbable and yet convincing. This type of decoration was much imitated later, but became more and more naturalistic until the porcelain itself was completely forgotten and by the last half of the nineteenth century it degenerated into the too realistic representation of inconsequent vegetation.

The first anchor mark (relief) was followed by the red (enamelled) anchor which shows perhaps the best period, and the one to which the finest of the botanical designs belongs. Little gilding was used during this period, but from about 1759 it was used much more lavishly and from then onwards the mark was a gold anchor. The Chelsea gilding is very soft and warm in colour and by comparison makes the highly burnished work of later times seem vulgar. Very little blue and white was made at Chelsea, which is regrettable as the little that is known is very beautiful, both in colour and glaze. The designs were mostly derivative from the Chinese or Japanese.

Little is known about the artists who worked for Chelsea, though there is much speculation on the matter. J. T. Smith in *Nollekins & his Times* makes Nollekins assert that his father (who was a painter) worked for this factory, and in the same paragraph Betew states that Sir James Thornhill and Paul Ferg did so also.

In 1770 the factory was bought up by Duesbury of Derby, and from then until 1784 is the Chelsea-Derby period.

The Derby factory seems to have been started about 1750. There is some uncertainty about the original owners of the works though Andrew Planché, John Heath and William Duesbury are mentioned in the early stages. Duesbury and Heath are known to have been the owners when Chelsea was bought up in 1770, and in 1779 Duesbury became sole manager.

The early Derby products are noticeable for the rather bluish glaze and general lightness of body. The figures, which were made in large numbers, are stiff and self-conscious beside those of Bow and Chelsea

LOWESTOFT MUG WITH SCALE BORDER, DECORATED WITH FLOWERS

From the collection of Mr. G. F. Hotblack

BOW, POSSIBLY WORCESTER, FIGURE OF A LADY IN A BLUE HAT WITH
YELLOW JACKET AND SKIRT STRIPED IN BLUE AND PUCE, C. 1765
From the collection of Mr. G. F. Hotblack

and though they have a certain charm they are not in the same class as the best groups from either of the other factories. Some of the early figures have been confused with those from Bow, but the colours, though similar, are apt to be blurred. The tableware was negligible in the early days, but later it was developed in a distinctive and formal manner, and after the amalgamation with Chelsea some really good work was produced.

The Chelsea-Derby tableware is some of the most perfect tea-table ware imaginable. It has all the delicacy and precision of fine craftsmanship, and the slight but fascinatingly satisfying decorations seem to symbolise all that the tea-table stood for in those leisured days. It is essentially English, and irresistibly conjures up pictures of Jane Austen and her friends, and the water colours of Thomas Girtin. The shapes of the teapots and cups show a real and practical appreciation of the art of tea drinking, and the wreaths, swags and delicate flower decorations only enhance the shapes themselves.

In 1784 the Chelsea works were closed down entirely but Derby continued until 1848, though its productions rapidly deteriorated in taste after the beginning of the nineteenth century. Mention must be made of the biscuit (unglazed) figures and groups which were made by this factory from about 1770 onwards. They are interesting as being the first of this type of figure to be made in England, in imitation of Sèvres. Unglazed porcelain has a sickly and smug quality which is not pleasant used in this way.

The Worcester factory was started in 1751 by a small company of men who set out to perfect a new porcelain formula incorporating the use of Cornish soapstone, which was first experimented with by William Cookworthy of Plymouth. It was probably due to this new body that early Worcester pieces are so much lighter and more clean-cut than most of their contemporaries. The early shapes are once again very reminiscent of silver work, and the glaze, which is of a fine even texture, is apt to be spoilt by the addition of cobalt in order to conform to the popular taste which admired the bluish tinge of the imported oriental wares.

As usual, the earliest productions were some of the most individual and attractive, and the first pieces are particularly crisp and fresh. Blue and white was very popular, and by 1759 the factory was in full swing making some of its best wares. The tea-sets of this period are charming with delicate, arabesque-like borders and sprinklings of flowers and insects in the Meissen tradition, but with fresh inspiration. A particularly delightful type of work about this time is the monochrome painting of Oriental landscapes in lilac, black or crimson.

Transfer printing was early practised at this factory (1757) and developed and used to a great extent, for the owners had a strong commercial sense. The designs were seldom original, but they were excellently placed in relation to the shapes of the wares, and the simple black, brown, purple

33

and sometimes red printings have definite charm, particularly when regarded as the cheap, everyday ware for general use. Robert Hancock's name is associated with most of the early engravings for these printings.

The Japanese influence was very strong at Worcester even from the earliest days, but it was well assimilated and freshly interpreted, and in the tableware particularly there was done some very pleasant work of this type in the early years. Later this mode of decoration deteriorated even more rapidly than most. The shapes of the tablewares are restrained, elegant (in the best sense) and serviceable, and show a sound appreciation of their purpose.

About 1670, the coloured grounds for which Worcester achieved such a name, were perfected and much used. Technically they are excellent, but as a type of decoration they never seem to be part and parcel of the

STAFFORDSHIRE (NEW HALL) PORCELAIN
Late eighteenth and early nineteenth centuries

34

'CHELSEA-DERBY' PORCELAIN
Table-ware made at Chelsea under the management of William Duesbury, c. 1775

body itself, and one is haunted by the horrible developments of the nine-teenth century which they foreshadow. Their gilding on the other hand was in excellent taste,. for those who like it. About 1780 the decline in taste really began, gently at first, but later in the wave of Victorian prosperity it rushed downwards.

This factory, alone of the early ones, has continued working until the present day, although inevitably its work deteriorated during the nineteenth century. But it still has a fine tradition of craftsmanship, and there is no reason why it should not produce some work of real interest in the future.

Thomas Turner of Worcester introduced the manufacture of porcelain to the works at Caughley in 1772, and from then until about 1814 porcelain was made, which is often extremely like some of the early Worcester. The Caughley body is less blue than Worcester, but in other ways is very like, and also contains soapstone.

Blue and gold was much used at this factory and some of the plain blue decoration of sprays and flowers is very charming in design and rich in colour.

Porcelain was made at Bristol as early as 1750, but the factory, owned by William Lowdin, was bought up by Worcester in 1752. The Lowdin Bristol and early Worcester pieces are not easily distinguishable, but on the whole the pieces now definitely attributed to Lowdin have a simpler

35

and more naive charm. The shapes were very derivative from silver-work as in early Worcester, but the paintings in colours were fresher and more interesting than the usual work from that factory.

In 1770 William Cookworthy set up his factory at Bristol for making hard-paste porcelain. This was taken over by Richard Champion in 1773 and in 1781 the patent rights were sold to a Staffordshire Company which started works at New Hall. Tebo (or Thibaud) who worked at Bow and Worcester, seems also to have worked at Bristol for Champion, and his hand is seen in the statuettes in the Meissen manner made at these works. The ordinary tableware, such as tea-sets, made by this factory were admirable and emphasise that individual and utilitarian tradition in manu-facture which is always to be found somewhere. Gilding was omitted for cheapness, but the results were often more distinguished without it. Simple sprays of flowers are scattered over practical and pleasant shapes, with sometimes simple ribbon or wreath borders.

Liverpool porcelain manufacture began in 1756, and is generally regarded as another offshoot of Worcester, on account of the fact that one of its workers, Podmore, is said to have passed on the knowledge of the use of soapstone which he brought from Worcester. The porcelain is somewhat greyish in colour, but there are some excellent pieces, notably jugs and mugs, painted in blue with a freeness very reminiscent of the delftware painters. There are also some charming transfer-printed wares in the Worcester manner, notably mugs and punch-bowls.

William Littler at Longton Hall made the first porcelain in Stafford-shire, and he is known to have been working there in 1752. His pro-ductions are noted for their raised leaf borders often painted in blue and for the rather heavy figure groups which are apt to be decorated with thick, not very attractive, colour and have the features picked out with theatrical harshness. The paste is glassy in character. It is known that Duesbury decorated ware for this factory, and it is believed that he bought up the works when they were closed down about 1760.

The small factory at Lowestoft, which made porcelain from 1757 until about 1803, has a reputation out of all proportion to its size or production, though none the less deserved. It had no pretensions to grandeur, and was almost entirely occupied with making utilitarian objects, which is probably the reason why its products seem to be such a personal expression of the people and their everyday life. Though the earliest pieces are nearly always decorated in underglaze blue with a strong Chinese influence in the designs, the character of the work is essentially peasant in its outlook, and this is more strongly noticeable in the later diaper-edge and flower sprinkled patterns more usually connected with this factory. It is interesting to note that this latter type of ware was actually copied in China, and later these flower painted pieces were also imitated in France. A number of mugs and inkstands are inscribed "A trifle from Lowestoft"

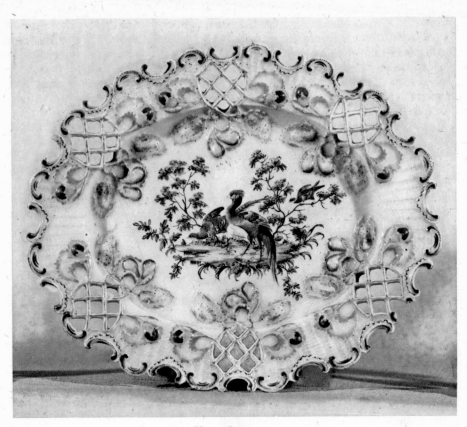

but otherwise the marks are vague and often merely imitated from other factories. The body is similar to Bow, but the glaze is much thinner ; typical borders are diapered in strong pink and brownish-red. The tea-sets are particularly charming and express all the friendliness of country cottages and village maidens. One of their chief decorators is thought to have been a Frenchman called Rose, a refugee from the French Revolution. At one time this factory did a flourishing trade with Holland and its failure and subsequent closing down was said to be due in part to the heavy loss sustained by the works when Napoleon captured Holland and destroyed a valuable store of Lowestoft porcelain in Rotterdam. In any case, it was an expensive factory to run, being far from both clay and coal.

Hard paste was made for a short time in Staffordshire at New Hall from 1781 in diminishing quantities until about 1810 it was superseded by a bone porcelain and the factory was closed in 1825. The early hard paste New Hall has distinct charm and shows a boldness of design which is striking in comparison with other contemporary work. Lustre was often used with a freedom reminiscent of some of the Maiolica painting, and the birds which appear are of quite a different type from those usually depicted.

With the end of the century a new era began and it was to be a dark age for pottery and porcelain in England. With increasing prosperity the demand for purely decorative wares grew rapidly, and the richer and more complicated the decoration the more popular it became. In the old days, as in the time of the Toft brothers, decorative ware was only made in the leisure moments of the potters or to mark some special occasion, and the light-hearted enjoyment of the makers is clearly to be seen in these personal expressions of the people. Now the same type of object began to be made in vast quantities for those who only wanted some expression of their opulence, and by those who worked for the money to be made rather than for the enjoyment of their work. This distortion of outlook overtook all the arts of that time, but some trace of the popular tradition survived in pottery and porcelain among the cheapest and most utilitarian wares.

BIRD FOUNTAIN
Earthenware with Copper Lustre Motif
Early 19th century

THE NINETEENTH CENTURY

With the beginning of the century we find that all the original porcelain factories, with the exception of Worcester, had either already closed down or were on the point of doing so. The early soft pastes of so much charm had been superseded by the bone-china which was perfected by the second Josiah Spode and came into general use, being sold in large quantities all over the world. The prosperity and commercialisation of the Potteries had a profound effect on the whole of Europe, and in fact the great Danish ceramic historian, Dr. Hannover, goes so far as to say that the development of all the ceramic arts of Europe was brought to a standstill by this great new English industry.

The mass produced bone-china was now so inexpensive that it virtually ousted pottery for general use, and when pottery was still made it usually strove to emulate porcelain shapes and colours with most unfortunate results.

It was left to Josiah Wedgwood to develop earthenware on suitable and sound lines, and to show that there was still a place for good design even in mass production. It is in the Wedgwood factory, more than any other, that we find the personal thread representing the needs and feelings of the people still persisting through this industrial revolution. It was Wedgwood who realised that, now the potter was no longer the artist but merely the mechanic or craftsman, it was necessary that the mechanic should have first class designs to guide him.

But before we review the work of the larger manufacturers of this century mention must be made of those smaller factories which came into being for a short time in the transition period. In 1796 a porcelain factory was set up at Pinxton in Derbyshire, and there was employed there one of the painters from the Derby works, William Billingsley, who subsequently founded the works at Nantgarw; therefore it is not surprising to find the work of these two factories very similar. The porcelain of both factories was very translucent, and the decorations were apt to be mainly imitative of Sèvres. The Pinxton works being the earlier of the two, its productions were inclined to be rather more unsophisticated and charming.

There had been a factory at Swansea since 1764, but it was only in 1814 that porcelain began to be made there, once more under Billingsley who was brought in by Dillwyn, the owner. The paste was again of the Nantgarw type, and much of the decoration was done in London.

Perhaps one of the greatest characteristics of the nineteenth century was the lack of assimilation of foreign influences. In earlier days we have noted how the continental and oriental designs were more the inspiration of the English potters than models for the mere copyist. Flowers and figures were translated into our own idiom and with our own ideas of colour to give new life, and one has the feeling that the potters and decorators had a full understanding and enjoyment of what they were doing. With the new outlook of the nineteenth century the continental and oriental designs were copied and elaborated because they were fashionable, and no longer were they the inspiration for designs of our own. This was of course mainly due to the fact that the potters were no longer artists, but commercial craftsmen who were caught up in the whirlwind of the new material age.

We find every sort of elaboration both of form and decoration ; and gilding, coloured grounds, embossments and fantastic shapes of all kinds flow in profusion from the Potteries. The craftsmanship is excellent but the taste is merely expensive. On the other hand, in the cheap transfer-decorated wares we often find some of the earlier naiveté and charm still lingering, for these cheap wares were made for the use of the people and not for the display of wealth.

Perhaps the two best known names which arose in the nineteenth century were those of Spode and Minton. As has been remarked before, the first Josiah Spode had come into notice at the end of the eighteenth century as a follower of Josiah Wedgwood and his cream-coloured earthenware, and later the second Josiah Spode sprang into fame by his perfecting of the bone-ware china. Some of the early Spode earthenware pieces are very similar to those of Wedgwood, and not only the shapes but also the decorations seem to have been copied freely. The early Spode porcelain was sometimes comparatively simple and pleasant in its decoration, but it soon took to the indiscriminate but fashionable use of gold and over-richness of pattern. Gilding in relief was particularly sumptuous in effect and is said to have been first done at this factory. Turquoise blue as a ground was also said to originate from here, and was much used at this time. A large amount of underglaze printing in blue (and later other colours) on both pottery and porcelain came from this factory as well as others, and in the first half of the century a large American market in this sort of ware developed. The favourite decorations were in the form of scenes of topical events and English landscapes. To this day much of this type of work is still exported to America, particularly for use in the larger universities and institutions there. The Minton factory achieved a world wide reputation for fine jewelled tableware, and certainly the texture and finish of their work was excellent, though the patronage of wealth once again brought over-ornamentation and gilding.

Worcester, early in the century produced some interesting and comparatively restrained Japanese designs, but later degenerated in the mid-Victorian period. They were particularly noted for their fine painting in imitation of Sèvres. From a technical point of view the work of this date was often very remarkable, but it was a mockery of the ceramic arts when plates and teapots began to be seen only as surfaces on which

TWO WEDGWOOD MUGS DESIGNED BY ERIC RAVILIOUS

Wedgwood Commemoration Mug. Etruria 1730 : Barlaston 1940

Edward VIII Coronation Mug dated 1937

FLOWER POT BY NORAH BRADEN
Oil painting by Beryl Sinclair

to paint realistic scenes of Windsor Castle, or still more realistic groups of expensive looking fruit. It was a tragic development, if one could so call it, from the charmingly stylised fruits and flowers painted a hundred years previously in the Chelsea works.

A more individual and therefore more interesting class of ware which flourished during the first quarter of the century was what is usually called Sunderland ware, made at Sunderland, Newcastle, and various places in the North. Lustre, particularly of a deep pink, was much used, in splashes and with crude dabs of enamel on topically printed earthenware mugs, jugs and bowls. As a contrast to the fine workmanship and sophisticated richness of the large Staffordshire firms of this date, this ware was crude in the extreme. But there is a wholesome vulgarity about it which is extremely attractive, and it has an intimacy with the ordinary people which is lacking in the more technically perfect but elaborately ostentatious productions of the larger factories.

Very little stoneware was made at this time that is worth mention; though in the early part of the century the Adams and Turner factories did produce some characteristic jugs decorated with embossed designs and dark brown enamelled necks. The Rockingham (Swinton) and Coalport works both produced notable examples of exuberant Victorian rococo. This was not without humour, though of the unconscious kind. Mention must be made here of Mason's "Ironstone" china which was patented early in the century and had a wide sale and popularity. Its chief virtue was its cheapness, and though it was also very durable this was a doubtful virtue owing to the usually hideous decoration. Blotting paper pink roses and brick red borders were typical of this ware.

The Great Exhibition of 1854 seemed to set the seal of approval on all the worst influences current at that time, and from then onwards there was an endless stream of grotesque "styles" in all the arts and crafts, and pottery did not escape. Indian, Greek and Moorish jostled each other in undigested confusion, and about 1860 the whole of Europe was swept by the vogue of Japanese art. Unfortunately, only the least worthy of Japanese art came to Europe ; the overdecorated Satsuma ware, as well as special lines made for export. It was not until half a century later that our potters found and were influenced by the restrained and beautiful shapes which were representative of the best in Japanese art.

William de Morgan must be cited as an important single figure of this time, in that he headed a reaction against the complicated and vulgar designs of the second half of the century. He produced some good work in the pre-Raphaelite manner. Clean coloured and clean shaped, and he showed a bold and pleasant use of lustre. But his influence was limited and of short duration.

The century closed in a welter of sumptuous distortion which gradually simmered down to a return to nature (as it was then thought to be) in

LUSTRE VASE BY WILLIAM DE MORGAN

L'Art Nouveau which now appears as a period of sickly and boneless sentimentality.

Yet all this time good pottery, and to a lesser degree good porcelain, was still being made for those who had the eyes to find it. For instance, much of the cheap earthenware turned out by Wedgwood was not only of excellent quality but it was well designed; and in many Victorian servants' halls the tableware was still representative of the best of English pottery traditions, whereas above stairs the tables groaned under the fashionable nightmares of ceramic art.

42

PRESENT DAY REACTIONS AND INFLUENCES

The new period of enlightenment which has lately been noticeable in the Pottery Industry is largely due to two causes. Firstly, there has been a fashionable revival and appreciation of all things pertaining to the last half of the eighteenth century. Secondly, the so-called studio potters have had an influence far beyond the few intellectuals who applauded their beginnings some twenty-five years ago. Taking the first cause, it is noticeable that in architecture the best of the modern houses are more closely related to those of the late eighteenth and early nineteenth centuries than to anything since, and this has reacted in all domestic taste. In the pottery world factories have searched their museums for early designs which have been adapted for present day purposes, and there is a general desire for the simple and serviceable prettiness of those early shapes. The florid exuberance of Victorian, and the wilting shapelessness of the Edwardian tablewares look hopelessly out of place in the modern house. The first is vulgarly self-conscious, and the second is depressingly insignificant. The new simplicity of architecture has made people unconsciously more aware of the importance of shape and therefore less demanding for richness of decoration. The worst tendencies nowadays are perhaps more towards undigested intellectualism rather than towards some equally undigested foreign influence.

The studio potters are perhaps responsible for most of the intellectual yearnings, but they have also taught much sound sense which had been forgotten for a century. They spoke of the right use of clay ; of the reason for a pot and its fitness for its purpose; of the importance of shape apart from decoration ; of the function of decoration to emphasise and not obscure a shape. They reaffirmed that the designer must also be a worker in clay, and must have a practical knowledge and experience of the nature of his material. This is now at last being understood by the factories, who are beginning to see that in mass production it is as important for the designer to know and understand the machinery as it is for the individual potter to know and understand his clay. The studio potters went to the East again for their inspiration but unlike the Victorians they sought out the best of oriental examples, and rejected the meretricious ware made to catch the eye of the traveller only. Perhaps they sometimes erred in being over-intellectual and exact in their interpretations, but at least they avoided vulgar distortion and grasped the fundamentals of pottery design.

Such people as Bernard Leach, W. Staite Murray and Michael Cardew, later followed by Miss Pleydell Bouverie, Miss Norah Braden and John Cole, have played a very real part in what looks like being a revival of the true art of pottery in this country. Bernard Leach worked for many years in Japan and has produced at his pottery at St. Ives some excellent

TWO JUGS AND A COVERED DISH BY BOURNE

work, noticeably stoneware. Michael Cardew has rediscovered English peasant pottery and has used slipware with particularly noticeable success in producing moderately priced and typically traditional oven and tableware.

Of necessity the work of the individual potters is much more expensive than that made by the large factories, but there is a very real place for both. It would seem that to-day the individual potter is more consciously a sculptor and an artist than of old, and his real triumphs are in the decorative pieces which have individual and personal beauty, and are the descendants of those show pieces of the Toft brothers and other workers of the seventeenth century.

But the advance of machinery cannot be ignored in any branch of industry, and just as furniture and textiles have become mass produced and sophisticated, so too must pottery do the same. The hand-made pots, together with hand-made furniture and textiles, can still be entirely lovely for those who have the leisure to make, or the money to acquire them, but there is no reason at all why beauty of a different kind should not spring from the machinery used for mass produced goods. The trouble comes when it is not understood that the beauty from machinery must be of an entirely different type from that of hand-made products. The one must not attempt to copy the other.

Some of the industrial potters in 1939 (at the beginning of the present war) were not only reproducing old designs, but were also beginning to use young designers of distinction who worked in the factories and thoroughly absorbed the processes of manufacture and understood the qualities of the materials for which they designed. Amongst these we find the interesting work of Eric Ravilious for Wedgwood's, and also the

44

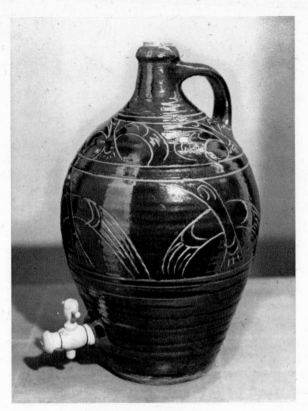

CIDER BOTTLE BY MICHAEL CARDEW

work of Graham Sutherland for William Brain. How different is the work of these men from that of the "designers" of the last century, who only saw a teapot as a good background for a realistic painting of a few plums or a plate as an opportunity to display an elegant sketch of a Stately Home of England.

But it is not only in decoration that the artist designer is making his mark on mass produced pottery, and we have for example in Keith Murray's beer mugs and jugs (designed for Wedgwood) simple undecorated shapes, which though essentially modern, have recaptured much of the understanding of clay which was so evident in the work of early English potters, and translated this knowledge into the idiom most suitable for mass production.

Salt-glaze, again, which was at one time the glory of English potting, has long fallen into disuse and until recently was principally to be found only in the manufacture of such articles as gingerbeer bottles and drain-

STONEWARE BOWLS MADE BY B. LEACH, NORAH BRADEN AND W. STAITE MURRAY

pipes. It is therefore interesting and inspiring to find such excellent work in this ware being produced by William Gordon at Chesterfield. The salt-glaze process is extremely inexpensive and economical in firing, and the wares so produced are very durable. The salt-glaze of the eighteenth century produced some of the loveliest and most typically English examples of ceramic art, but it was superseded by Wedgwood's cream earthenware which for domestic purposes had advantages over the salt-glaze. However, with greater knowledge and improved methods it now seems as though salt-glaze has special properties which may reinstate it as one of the most useful and charming types of ware. William Gordon's work shows a full appreciation of these special properties as well as a fine understanding of the salt-glaze tradition in this country, and it is to be hoped that he has opened up a new future for this typically English process of manufacture.

It is interesting and heartening to see to-day in the cheap stoneware jugs and kitchen pots made by Joseph Bourne of Denby, the direct descendants of those lovely jugs and pots made in the fourteenth and fifteenth centuries by our early potters. The texture and finish of Bourne's productions are indeed mechanically very different from those of the early potters, but the generosity and humour of the shapes, and the sound understanding of the purposes for which the vessels are made, are the same to-day as they were six hundred years ago.

46

CONCLUSION

We have now briefly traced the history of English pottery and porcelain through some six centuries, and coming to the present day it seems that we can end on a note of optimism for the future. This is an industry which has its natural roots in Britain, and since the earliest days the personal thread which has been particular to this country, has always persisted for those who cared to look for it. As each new process was perfected the inspiration then shifted to yet another channel, absorbing as it went the various foreign influences which crossed its path. With the nineteenth century it seemed as though for a time our national genius had been smothered by too much success and prosperity, but now it seems that new life has come to the Industry.

The studio potters have brought back to us the personal charm of the individual potter's craft, and have shown their awareness of the traditions of English ceramics in relation to foreign influences. They have absorbed those influences in the fullest sense and interpreted them in our native idiom. At the same time the industrial potters seem to be awakening to the fact that they must move forward again, and that future success now lies in ability to use the new machinery and processes as an inspiration to further effort and not to regard them as a quick and cheap way of reproducing the work of the past. It is too easy to criticise the present and mourn the passing of old methods and fashions. We must go forward or die, and provided we continue to build on the solid foundations of the past and keep in sight the needs of the people of this country, we cannot go far wrong ; and the future should hold much in store for this most indigenous of British industries.

SALTGLAZE WARE BY WILLIAM GORDON

BOW   CHELSEA

CHELSEA-DERBY   DERBY   LONGTON HALL

CAUGHLEY   WORCESTER

PLYMOUTH & BRISTOL   MINTON

SOME EXAMPLES OF THE EARLY MARKS ON ENGLISH PORCELAIN

It is impossible here to give a comprehensive list of English porcelain marks as these are so very numerous and various. All that has been attempted is to indicate the most obviously important, without going into the date variations of the factories. Certain marks, such as Lowestoft, Swansea, etc. are often self-evident by having the name in full, when the pieces from these factories are marked at all.